Breaking Free

Her Daily Journal To Freedom

January

Shanicka Scarbrough, MD

Printed in the United States of America
First Printing, 2017

ISBN: 1981487654
ISBN-13: 978-1981487653

Scriptures taken from the Holy Bible, English Standard Version®

DEDICATION

This book is dedicated to the women who have been burdened by their thoughts, feelings, and circumstances beyond their control. Know that you have been given the tools to break free!

ACKNOWLEDGEMENTS

Most of this journal was written during my visit to South Africa. Our church, BOSS Church of Sacramento, pastored by my husband, Rev. Darryl Scarbrough, got a chance to enrich ourselves in the lives and culture of those from Cape Town and Johannesburg. What struck me the most and to my core being, was that although on the surface, the South Africans looked free, they were still being oppressed by a seen and unseen racial caste system much like minority populations in the United States. Over half of the population is living in poverty and many are unable to afford proper housing or a decent education for their children. Despite this, over 90% of the population are Christians and the spirit of faith and hope is evident in all that they say and do. I would like to pray for our brother and sisters in South Africa, that they soon break free and arise the kings and queens God intended them to be.

Week 1
January 1st-7th

Break Free of Toxic Relationships

Relationships are a tough thing to navigate. To not only be mindful of those in your life, but to be able to accept and love them unconditionally through the storm as well as the sunshine. We do this with the ultimate goal of living harmoniously while we continue to have breath in our bodies. Trust, I know 1st hand that this can often times be a lofty ambition, but one that is definitely worth fighting for.

When I speak about relationships, I am not just speaking of how you interact with your significant other. I am extending this to all those whom you come in contact with, including but not limited to your family, your friends, and your coworkers or classmates. Unfortunately, whether you are related by blood or brought together by your place of employment, school or social environment, do understand that everyone who smiles at you and laughs with you, does not have your best interest at heart. When that so-called friend deceives you, or a family member maliciously speaks your name, or a coworker talks about you behind your back, it's becomes vital that we seek God for discernment and take it a step further, by letting those people go. You do not need toxic people in your life.

Letting go could be one of the hardest things you could possibly do, especially if they are a member of your family or counting the years that you have not been friends is easier than counting the number of years you have been BFFs (best friends forever). If that person goes against your moral values and consistently ignores your feelings of discomfort with the things they say or do, then it's time to let them go. If they intentionally hurt you and secretly or openly wishes ill will on your behalf, guess what, it's time for them to go.

I am not saying that you will not have arguments or disagreement with the ones you love and if you do to kick them to the curb for not seeing your point of view. No, not at all! What I am saying is that in order for you to continue to grow closer in your walk with Christ, you must forgive those who have hurt you and come to the realization that it is ok to love them from afar. Perhaps, at a later date, God will draw them nearer to you, and reinstate them in your life. You can be prepared to open your arms and help them through their journey, but also be prepared if this never happens, and be ok with the latter.

"What if I am the toxic person?" you may ask. That is a valid question and great insight on your part. In order for you to truly be like Christ and follow in his ways, then you must humble yourself and ask yourself why you are deciding to be that way. Yes, I said decide. How you interact with other people is a decision, an act of free will. Start today by choosing to love and show love as Christ showed us, regardless of our own messes and issues. He continues to draw us closer to Him so that He can wash us of our sins and immorality, giving us the gift of righteousness that we most certainly do not deserve but He gives it freely anyhow.

My Prayer For You

Heavenly Father, you are amazing and we are careful to give you the praise in all we do. Thank you for being our BFF! Lord, I come to you on behalf of my sister, I pray that she begins to seek and desire to become more like you, to exhibit kindness, patience, humility, compassion and most of all, love to the people that you have charged to be in her life. Lord, we pray for wisdom and discernment and seek out relationships that are pleasing in your sight. Remove those who do not have our best interest at heart, who's hearts are hardened against us, who speak our names with contempt. We pray to love them anyhow just as you love them despite their feelings towards us. Lord protect our hearts against those who come against us. We pray our lives will be a lamp that draws them closer to you. In the mighty name of Jesus, Amen!

January 1st (New Year's Day)

Do not be unequally yoked with unbelievers. For what partnership has righteousness with lawlessness? Or what fellowship has light with darkness?

1 Corinthians 6:14

Today's Prayer:

Self-Reflection:

Epiphany:

January 2nd

Do not be deceived:
"Bad company ruins good morals."

1 Corinthians 15:33

Today's Prayer:

Self-Reflection:

Epiphany:

January 3rd

Make no friendship with a man given to anger, nor go with a wrathful man, lest you learn his ways and entangle yourself in a snare.
Proverbs 22:24-25

Today's Prayer:

Self-Reflection:

Epiphany:

January 4th

Whoever walks with the wise becomes wise, but the companion of fools will suffer harm.
Proverbs 13:20

Today's Prayer:

Self-Reflection:

Epiphany:

January 5th

Two are better than one, because they have a good reward for their toil. For if they fall, one will lift up his fellow.
Ecclesiastes 4:9-10

And though a man might prevail against one who is alone, two will withstand him—a threefold cord is not quickly broken.
Ecclesiastes 4:12

Today's Prayer:

Self-Reflection:

Epiphany:

January 6th

Faithful are the wounds of a friend;
profuse are the kisses of an enemy.
Proverbs 27:6

Today's Prayer:

Self-Reflection:

Epiphany:

January 7th

Put on then, as God's chosen ones, holy and beloved, compassionate hearts, kindness, humility, meekness, and patience, bearing with one another and, if one has a complaint against another, forgiving each other; as the Lord has forgiven you, so you also must forgive. 14 And above all these put on love, which binds everything together in perfect harmony. Corinthians 3:12-14

Today's Prayer:

____

____

____

____

____

____

____

____

____

Self-Reflection:

Epiphany:

Week 2
January 8th-14th

Break Free of Depression, Anxiety, and Fear

When I was a child, I was afraid of the dark. If there were shadows in my room from the crack of light shining through my bedroom window, or my closet door was cracked, I would completely freak out, thinking there was something nefarious lurking in the shadows. But I would never call out to my mom because I wanted to handle it on my own for fear that I would be ridiculed or continuously told by my mother that "nothing is there...go to sleep!" She didn't understand my plight.

So despite this irrational feeling, the fear and the anxiety would grip me and in an effort to shut it all out, I would grab my comforter (even in the summer time) and pull it over my head, hiding from the monsters I was sure were lurking in the dark to attack me. I would be so terrified that I would tremble and sweat from the anticipation of something terrible happening to me. I was trapped in my own living nightmare every other night. In my mind, if I covered every part of my body, head to toe, then the monsters would not be able to see me and they would disappear. Every night this operation "worked" as I buried myself under the covers where I would find comfort and was able to finally rest.

Jesus wants you to experience this kind of rest ALL OF THE TIME. He does not want your circumstances to define who you are and foster fear of what's to come affecting your mood and well being. Jesus covers us in much the same way my comforter would cover me, shielding me from the unseen monsters. When we accept Him as our Lord and Savior, He moves on our behalf, protecting us and providing comfort in our times of fear, distress, depression, or anxiety. He promises that He will never leave us and when He died on the cross for our sins, the blood that he shed stretches out like a warm comforter of protection that covers us spiritually from head to toe.

No matter what your situation or circumstance looks like, remember that God is bigger than any of your problems. When we are connected to this covering, we are protected by our living God. The bible says to be anxious for nothing, but pray with thanksgiving or a grateful heart letting your requests and desires be made known to God. This is an opportunity to lay all of your cares, your sadness and/or depression, your grieviences, your anxiety, your frustrations, your trials, and your burdens, on the one who has the power to actually change them. What an amazing revelation! Our Father can change any situation for our good, simply because we are His children and His love for us covers all.

What does that look like for you? Know this with confidence, you are able to break free from this bondage of mental and emotional anguish by accepting God's truths (his living word as recorded in the bible) and implementing your faith that God will work it all out in your favor simply because you love Him. Isn't that good news?!?

My Prayer for You:

Heavenly Father, we come to you with humble hearts and open minds. We invite the Holy Spirit to wash over us, cleanse us of our sins, and we pray your blood covers us like our favorite blanket or comforter, releasing us from worry, doubt, sadness, and feelings of low self worth. Remind us that you are King of Kings and as your beloved children we inherit all of your promises. Lord, comfort us in our times of need, wipe away every tear, show yourself strong in our lives. Thank you for your hedge of protection and brand new mercies every morning. These blessings we ask in the mighty name of Jesus. Amen!

January 8th

The steadfast love of the Lord never ceases; his mercies never come to an end; they are new every morning; great is your faithfulness.
"The Lord is my portion," says my soul,
"therefore I will hope in him."
Lamentations 3:18-29

Today's Prayer:

Self-Reflection:

Epiphany:

January 9th

It is the Lord who goes before you. He will be with you; he will not leave you or forsake you. Do not fear or be dismayed.
Deuteronomy 31:8

Today's Prayer:

Self-Reflection:

Epiphany:

January 10th

When the righteous cry for help, the Lord hears and delivers them out of all their troubles. The Lord is near to the brokenhearted and saves the crushed in spirit.

Psalm 34:17-18

Today's Prayer:

Self-Reflection:

Epiphany:

January 11th

I waited patiently for the Lord; he inclined to me and heard my cry. He drew me up from the pit of destruction, out of the miry bog and set my feet upon a rock, making my steps secure.
He put a new song in my mouth, a song of praise to our God.
Psalm 40:1-3

Today's Prayer:

Self-Reflection:

Epiphany:

January 12th

Why are you cast down, O my soul, and
why are you in turmoil within me?
Hope in God; for I shall again praise him,
my salvation and my God.
Psalm 42:11

Today's Prayer:

Self-Reflection:

Epiphany:

January 14th

Blessed be the God and Father of our Lord Jesus Christ, the Father of mercies and God of all comfort, 4 who comforts us in all our affliction, so that we may be able to comfort those who are in any affliction, with the comfort with which we ourselves are comforted by God.

2 Corinthians 1:3-4

Today's Prayer:

Self-Reflection:

Epiphany:

January 14th

For I am sure that neither death nor life, nor angels nor rulers, nor things present nor things to come, nor powers, nor height nor depth, nor anything else in all creation, will be able to separate us from the love of God in Christ Jesus our Lord.

Romans 8:38-39

Today's Prayer:

Self-Reflection:

Epiphany:

Week 3

January 15th-21st

Break Free of the Busy Body

As a child, I used to love to play the telephone game. It would just crack me up to see how misconstrued the message would be at the end when the final person in the chain had to relay what was supposed to be the originating message. If you have ever played this game, then you know that the message was NEVER the same and barely a skeleton of what that initial person whispered in the next person's ear. Why is that? Do we only hear what we want to hear and relay only that message? Do we have "selective hearing?" Or are we intentionally changing the message so that in the end we could all share in a good laugh?

Little did I know that this silly game as kids was an imitation of what happens in real life when we decide to participate in gossip. How many times have you said or heard someone say "Girl, did you hear..," or "Girl, give me the tea!" or worse yet, "You didn't hear this from me, but..." One person starts off the story and in the end the story has completely shifted and changed, so much so that the end product has literally ruined the subject of the story's life. Some people only relay a part of the message that they want the other person to know, or they may intentionally change the story to hurt the other person, but the bottom line is the truth is no where to be found and that person who is the "headliner" has suffered a great injustice simply because we decided to be busy bodies in their life story.

This is not how God intended us to behave. Your tongue should not have the power to impact someone else's life, but unfortunately it does. It's all gravy when it's someone else whom we are talking about, but let the subject shift to us, then we are all up in arms and ready to fight! It does not feel good to be the topic of discussion, let alone, the topic of misinformation. Worse yet, the information that is so carelessly spread by loose tongues can actually be detrimental to that person's life, mental health, and possibly physical well-being. This is not of God and God gives plenty of warnings to us about being busy bodies.

Even if you are not the one spreading lies, if you sit and listen to it, you are just as guilty as if you were the one speaking it. If you want to improve your stature in this God-forsaken telephone game, you need to make it uncomfortable for someone to be able to come to you with poison from their lips.

My mother used to ask me this simple question, "Did you hear it from the horse's mouth?" If the information that is being spread about a person did not come directly from their mouth to your ears and is coming by way of a 2nd, 3rd or 4th source, then it needs to be regarded as hearsay and not as the truth and disregarded for what it is, or possibly what it is not. We, especially as women, should carry the desire to want to uplift our sisters, and not tear them down. Our lips should drip with praise, encouragement, and support of one another as we all try to live this thing called life. God has charged us to love one another as He has loved us. This can only happen by guarding our words carefully as to not fan the flame of negativity. Our words should be like water on the seed of encouragement that will help the person blossom into who God has called them to be.

My Prayer for You:

Thank you Lord for being the Great I Am. You love us enough to know the exact number of hairs on our heads! What a mighty show of love! Thank you for not holding our sins against us. Who are we to hold someone else's sins against them? Lord, we come asking you to remove the busy body in us, that we do not have the desire to participate in such destructive behavior, that we learn to bridle our tongues, and not speak evil against one another. Give us a compassionate heart, that we may not judge those who sin against you, that we desire and choose love above all else. It's in the mighty name of Jesus we pray, Amen!

January 15th

Let no corrupting talk come out of your mouths,
but only such as is good for building up,
as fits the occasion, that it may give
grace to those who hear.
Ephesians 4:29

Today's Prayer:

Self-Reflection:

Epiphany:

January 16th

You shall not spread a false report. You shall not join hands with a wicked man to be a malicious witness.
Exudas 23:1

Today's Prayer:

Self-Reflection:

Epiphany:

January 17th

For lack of wood the fire goes out, and where there is no whisperer, quarreling ceases. As charcoal to hot ember and wood to fire, so is a quarrelsome man for kindling strife.
The words of a whisperer are like delicious morsels; they go down into the inner parts of the body. Like the glaze covering an earthen vessel are fervent lips with an evil heart.
Proverbs 26:20-23

Today's Prayer:

Self-Reflection:

Epiphany:

January 18th

Set a guard, O Lord, over my mouth; keep watch over the door of my lips! Do not let my heart incline to any evil, to busy myself with wicked deeds in company with men who work iniquity.
Psalm 141:3-4

Today's Prayer:

Self-Reflection:

Epiphany:

January 19th

Do not speak evil against one another, brothers. The one who speaks against a brother or judges his brother, speaks evil against the law and judges the law. But if you judge the law, you are not a doer of the law but a judge.

James 4:11

Today's Prayer:

Self-Reflection:

Epiphany:

January 20th

Death and life are in the power of the tongue,
and those who love it will eat its fruits.
Proverbs 18:21

Today's Prayer:

Self-Reflection:

Epiphany:

January 21st

When words are many, transgression is not lacking, but whoever restrains his lips is prudent.
Proverbs 10:19

Today's Prayer:

Self-Reflection:

Epiphany:

Self-Reflection

Epiphany

Week 4
January 22nd-28th

Break Free From Addiction

I was given a pass by my doctor to eat whatever I wanted for 3 weeks straight. Now for the average person, this sounds like paradise! But to me it was the beginning of a sweet, delicious, nightmare. I was given this pass because for months I had been suffering from stomach aches, bloating and gas whenever I ate not only dairy but pasta as well as anything breaded. The concern was for a gluten sensitivity caused by celiac disease and the only way to determine if this was my problem, I had to eat regular food including the ones that gave me the trouble. This would cause inflammation that the doctor could actually see. If I continued to eat my gluten-free and dairy free diet then the doctor would not be able to make a diagnosis.

Well, I went all in! I enjoyed "regular" spaghetti again, various types of breads and sandwiches, cakes and pastries, all of things I dumped from my diet previously all in the name of getting to the bottom of my illness. Yes, my stomach was killing me the entire time but overtime, I ignored the pain and relished on how good the food tasted instead.

Thanks to this little experiment MONTHS ago, I am still struggling to this day with the extra 15 lbs that I have added, even after the doctor gave me a clean bill of health. The problem is, all of the foods I had eliminated initially, I had eliminated for good reason. Not only were they making me sick, they were also making me overweight, impacting my overall health. These foods also have substances (sugar being one of them) that is addictive and they activate the pleasure center in our brains, causing us to override the detrimental effects they have on our bodies.

Your addiction may not be food, it may be gambling, drugs, alcohol, sex, or pornography. Whatever the addiction, the mechanism is the same. Addiction is defined as a brain disorder characterized by the compulsive engagement in rewarding stimuli despite adverse consequences. Your brain and body wants what makes it feel good, it get to a point where it NEEDS to feel good and it becomes the most important thing to you, regardless if that thing that makes you feel good is actually bad for you.

It is not by accident that we have a God who came down on earth in the human form, and endured every type of suffering we could imagine and resisted the need to make it all go away and just feel good. Our savior was tempted on a regular by satan and, thankfully, He never gave in to the temptations. Because of this, God will never allow us to be tempted beyond what we are capable of and if we do fall, He provides us a way out. With the help of God, you can be delivered from your addiction. You just have to chose Him. Release your addiction to Him today and seek the help you need (rehabilitation, counseling, dietician, etc.) to rid yourself once and for all of the thing that has taken hold of your life. Reclaim yourself in Christ Jesus.

My Prayer for You:

Our God in Heaven, hallowed be thy name, thy kingdom come, your will be done, in earth as it is in Heaven. We pray right now in the name of Jesus that we bind the spirits of addiction, dependence, fixation and obsession, and we loose healing over our minds and spirits, breaking free from the strongholds of this type of oppression. Thank you for knowing what it feels like to be tempted and overcoming, give us your overcoming power, do not let anything that is unlike you grab hold of our will. We break these chains in the mighty name of Jesus, Amen!

January 22nd

No temptation has overtaken you that is not common to man. God is faithful, and he will not let you be tempted beyond your ability, but with the temptation he will also provide the way of escape, that you may be able to endure it. Therefore, my beloved, flee from idolatry.

1 Corinthians 10:13-14

Today's Prayer:

Self-Reflection:

Epiphany:

January 23rd

Or do you not know that the unrighteous will not inherit the kingdom of God? Do not be deceived: neither the sexually immoral, nor idolaters, nor adulterers, nor men who practice homosexuality, nor thieves, nor the greedy, nor drunkards, nor revilers, nor swindlers will inherit the kingdom of God. And such were some of you. But you were washed, you were sanctified, you were justified in the name of the Lord Jesus Christ and by the Spirit of our God.
1 Corinthians 6:9-11

Today's Prayer:

____

____

____

____

____

____

____

____

Self-Reflection:

Epiphany:

January 24th

"All things are lawful for me," but not all things are helpful. "All things are lawful for me," but I will not be dominated by anything.
1 Corinthians 6:12

Today's Prayer:

Self-Reflection:

Epiphany:

January 25

For the grace of God has appeared, bringing salvation for all people, 12 training us to renounce ungodliness and worldly passions, and to live self-controlled, upright, and godly lives in the present age, waiting for our blessed hope, the appearing of the glory of our great God and Savior Jesus Christ, who gave himself for us to redeem us from all lawlessness and to purify for himself a people for his own possession who are zealous for good works.

Titus 2:11-14

Today's Prayer:

Self-Reflection:

Epiphany:

January 26th

For we do not have a high priest who is unable to sympathize with our weaknesses, but one who in every respect has been tempted as we are, yet without sin. Let us then with confidence draw near to the throne of grace, that we may receive mercy and find grace to help in time of need.
Hebrews 4:15-16

Today's Prayer:

Self-Reflection:

Epiphany:

January 27th

Watch and pray that you may not enter into temptation. The spirit indeed is willing, but the flesh is weak.
Matthew 26:41

Today's Prayer:

Self-Reflection:

Epiphany:

January 28th

Do not love the world or the things in the world. If anyone loves the world, the love of the Father is not in him. For all that is in the world—the desires of the flesh and the desires of the eyes and pride of life —is not from the Father but is from the world. And the world is passing away along with its desires, but whoever does the will of God abides forever.

1 John 2:15-17

Today's Prayer:

Self-Reflection:

Epiphany:

Week 5
January 29th-31st

Break Free From Overworking

Women tend to be the best multi-taskers there are known to mankind. We have an uncanny ability to juggle multiple things at once, more often than not, excelling at the tasks at hand. It may seem to some that this "gene" is passed down from generation to generation where women wear multiple "hats" indicative of the role she has currently stepped into.

You know what I'm talking about. We are mothers, wives, daughters, sisters, ministry leaders, employees, entrepreneurs and small business owners, lovers, counselors, stay-at-home moms, best friends, the boss lady, or whatever else you would like to call us. We keep the house clean, meals prepared, the company afloat, the finances straight, the boo-boos fixed, the hair braided, the refrigerator and pantries stocked, a shoulder available for perpetual leaning, and an ear open for late night chats. We do it all! And we do it well! But sometimes, we do it to our own detriment.

We work and work and work to keep a roof over the house, to increase our stature in society, to increase our wealth, to provide for our families. At the surface, this increased need to accumulate things and to protect and serve our loved ones, we must be careful to not make the love of these things bigger than our love for God. This becomes what we call idolatry and if we are not conscious to renew our strength in the Lord, to learn to listen to do God's will, and to take intentional rest, then we reap the physical, mental, and spiritual consequences of our actions. You have to be "tapped in". What you don't want to do is be working on a life not in accordance to what God wants for your life, or unfortunately, your work will all be in vain, as well as take a serious tole on your mind, body and spirit.

Your expectations of where you are can be disappointing when you look at it from your perspective, especially when you are trying to accomplish it all in your own might. That is one trick of the devil, keep you busy with busy work and your eyes off Christ, and to burden your spirit, constantly telling you that you are not good enough, you haven't accomplished enough, you do not earn enough, you are not famous enough. therefore, you are not worthy.

This is farthest from the truth and its not time to silence the enemy once and for all. In Christ, you are more than what you do, you are more than your title, you are more than what is in your bank account. You are a child of the most high, and when you put God 1st, seek his will for life, and act on what he has revealed to you, it is then and only then when you begin to walk in your purpose, so that you may draw someone else closer to him (bear fruit). You will take pleasure in your "work" as it is God's gift to you.

My Prayer for You:

Heavenly Father, we come to you with thanksgiving in our hearts. We love and adore who you are, the Great I Am. Thank you Lord for impregnating each of us with a purpose. I pray for every sister that she begins to experience rest in you, that she no longer tries to go through life in her own strength, ignoring your promises. May she find strength in you, working towards building your kingdom, putting you above all things material. It's in the mighty name of Jesus we pray, Amen!

January 29th

Unless the Lord builds the house, those who build it labor in vain. Unless the Lord watches over the city, the watchman stays awake in vain. It is in vain that you rise up early and go late to rest, eating the bread of anxious toil; for he gives to his beloved sleep.

Psalm 127:1-2

Today's Prayer:

Self-Reflection:

Epiphany:

January 30th

I perceived that there is nothing better for them than to be joyful and to do good as long as they live; also that everyone should eat and drink and take pleasure in all his toil—this is God's gift to man.
Ecclesiastes 3:12-13

Let the favor of the Lord our God be upon us, and establish the work of our hands upon us; yes, establish the work of our hands!
Psalm 90:17

Today's Prayer:

Self-Reflection:

Epiphany:

January 31st

He who loves money will not be satisfied with money, nor he who loves wealth with his income; this also is vanity.
Ecclesiastes 5:10

Keep your life free from love of money, and be content with what you have, for he has said, "I will never leave you nor forsake you."
Hebrews 13:5

Today's Prayer:

Self-Reflection:

Epiphany:

Self-Reflection

Epiphany

ABOUT THE AUTHOR

Dr. Shanicka Scarbrough (aka America's Favorite Family Doctor) graduated from the University of Illinois College of Medicine in 2009 and completed her family medicine residency program at Advocate Christ Medical Center in 2012. Since then, she has gained invaluable experience as a board-certified family medicine physician and has had the privilege of owning and operating a private medical practice. She now teaches other physicians and physicians-in-training how to start their own medical practice with her bestselling book, The Lunchtime Physician Entrepreneur, and her live virtual courses in the Road to Private Practice Academy.

Having hosted the The DivaMD radio show on Urban Broadcast Media, and continuing to contribute to a variety of other platforms on television and social media, she speaks in various educational settings and travels internationally, including to Haiti and South Africa, to extend her knowledge, skills, and expertise across the globe.

Dr. Shanicka has also released her 1st anthology, As the Wind Blows, a collection of seven women's stories of weakness, including her own, and how they overcame life's obstacles. Dr. Shanicka's mission is to be transparent about her life in hopes that sharing her testimonies will help bring others closer to God.

The Her Daily Journal Monthly Series was a God-given vision to release one interactive journal a month with a new topic to foster a deeper understanding of self and increase the reader's relationship with Christ by providing biblical application to every day life. Be on the look out for the February journaling experience!

To connect, visit her website at
www.DrShanicka.com